level 4

TECHNIC LESSONS

by JAMES BASTIEN

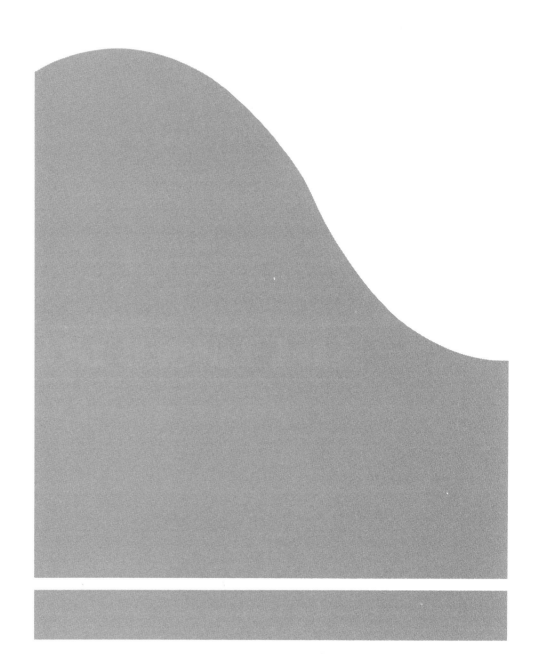

KJOS WEST · Neil A. Kjos. Jr. Publisher · San Diego. California

TO THE TEACHER

TECHNIC LESSONS, Level 4, is designed to be used simultaneously with **PIANO LESSONS, Level 4** (©*1976 KJOS WEST, San Diego, California, Ed. No. WP5*). It may also be used with any piano course.

DYNAMICS Unless indicated, the dynamics are to be suggested by the teacher. On each repeat of the exercise, have the student use a different dynamic level.

TEMPO Direct the student to play each exercise in three tempos: slow, medium and fast. On each repeat, have the student use a different tempo.

TOUCH Some exercises have specific directions to practice both legato and staccato. Many of the legato exercises (those with slurs) may also be played staccato at the teacher's discretion.

TRANSPOSITION Transposition is indicated for some exercises. Additional transposition for these exercises may be suggested at the teacher's discretion.

The goal of **TECHNIC LESSONS** is to develop hand and finger coordination and facility, and to develop ease and control at the keyboard. A variety of keyboard experiences is provided to give the student a basic foundation in elementary fundamentals.

Suggested Use of Materials with "PIANO LESSONS, Level 4."

SHEET MUSIC from **Level Four Solos** may be assigned to the student at the teacher's discretion.

At this point in the **BASTIEN PIANO LIBRARY**, the student has the background to go on to standard piano literature and supplementary materials in Levels 5 and 6 listed on the back cover.

ISBN 0-8497-5014-8

TO THE STUDENT

The studies in this book are designed to help you play the piano with ease and control. Allow time each day for technic practice. You might use these studies as warm-ups before beginning to practice your pieces.

Think of these three points often.

HEIGHT — Sit up high enough to reach the keys easily. Your wrists and forearms should be in a *straight line* over the keys.

POSTURE — Sit up *straight* in front of the center of the piano. Place your feet flat on the floor.

HAND POSITION — When playing the piano, hold your fingers in a nice *curved shape*.

CONTENTS

FIVE FINGER PATTERNS

1.

1st time—*legato*
2nd time—*staccato*

2.

legato—staccato

3.

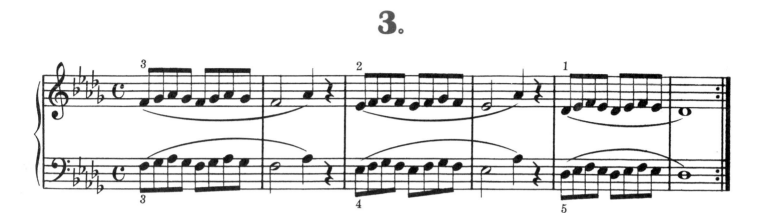

4.

5.

"OVERLAPPING" PEDAL STUDIES

1.

2.

PEDAL ETUDE

TWO OCTAVE SCALE STUDIES

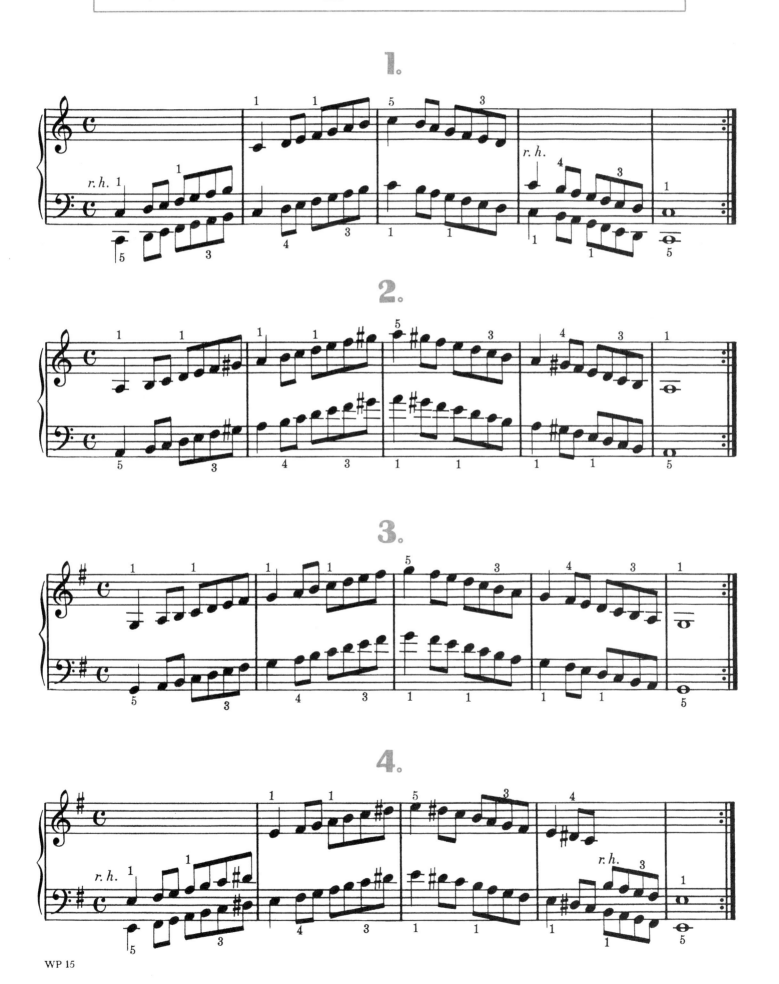

FINGER EXTENSION STUDIES ~ 7THS

CLIMBING A HILL

CLIMBING UP A TREE

CLIMBING DOWN A TREE

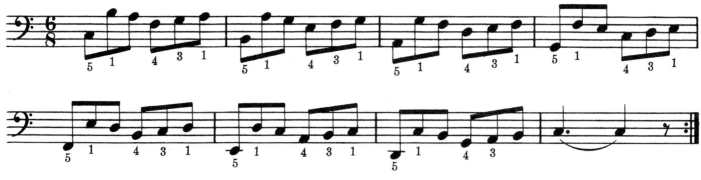

DOODLING

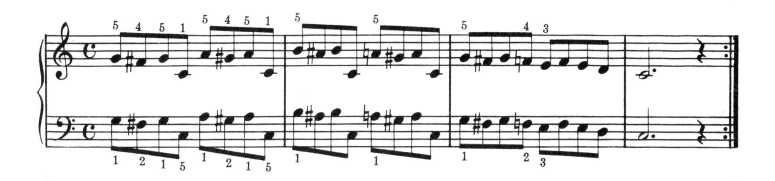

ROTO ROOTER

TILT~A~WHIRL

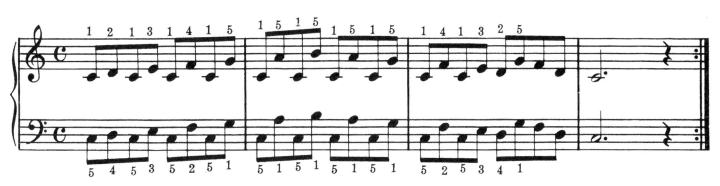

FIRST INVERSION TRIAD STUDIES

1.

2.

FIRST INVERSION ETUDE

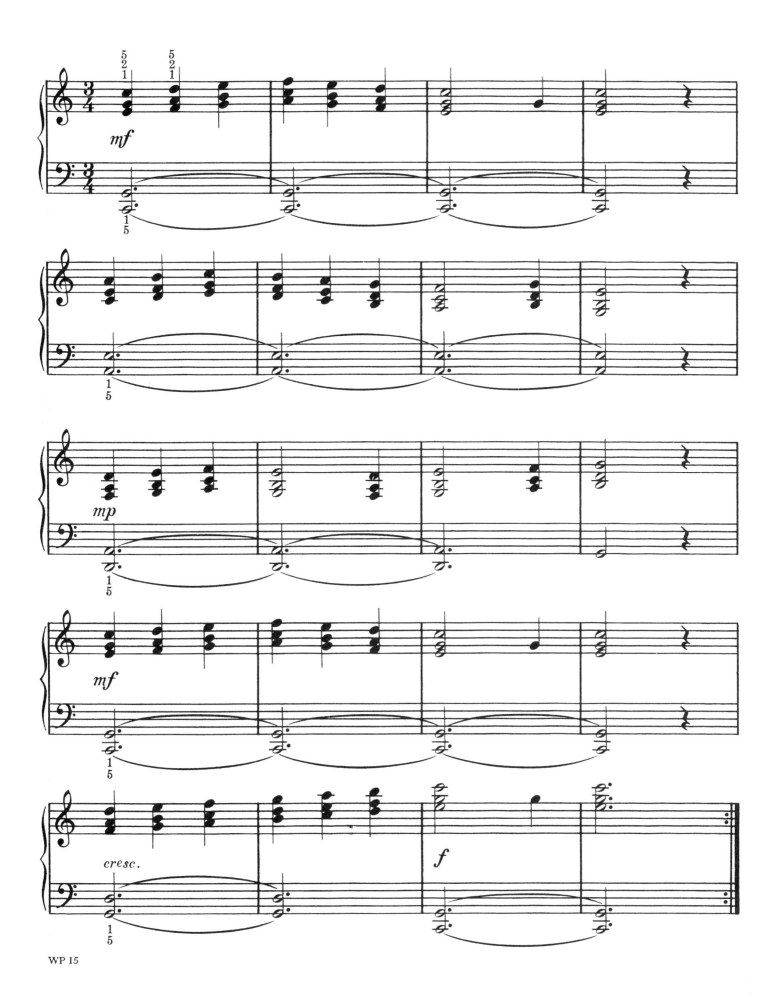

FINGER EXTENSION STUDIES~ OCTAVES

POGO STICK PARADE

ON THE TRAMPOLINE

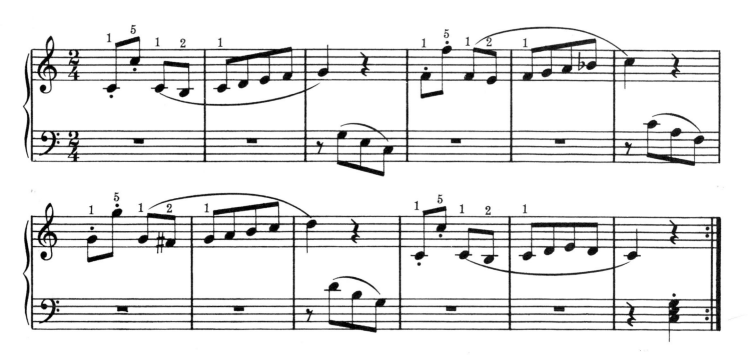

FINGER INDEPENDENCE STUDIES

1.

2.

Practice hands separately first, then together.

3.

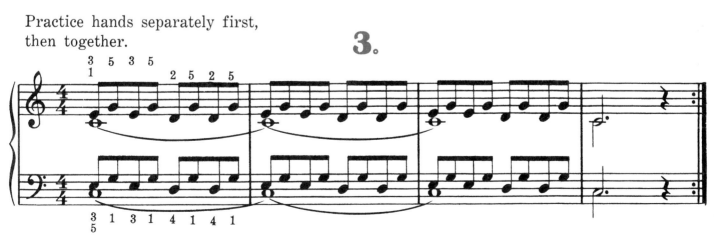

SECOND INVERSION TRIAD STUDIES

Practice hands separately first, then together.

WARM-UPS

SECOND INVERSION ETUDE

FINGER INDEPENDENCE STUDIES

1.

Hold all fingers down
except the one playing.

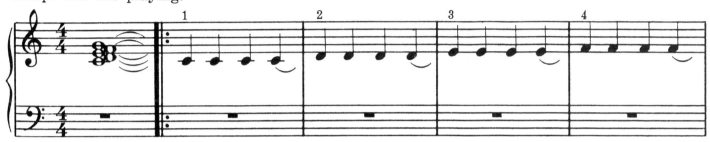

2.

Hold all fingers down
except the one playing.

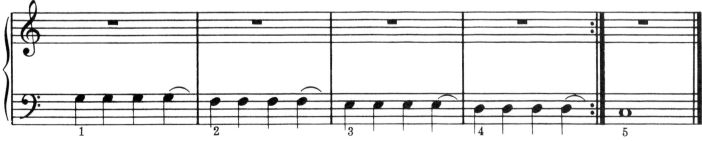

SIXTEENTH NOTE RHYTHM STUDY

legato—staccato

WRIST STACCATO STUDIES

1.

2.

3.

4.

TRILL STUDY

Transpose to other keys.

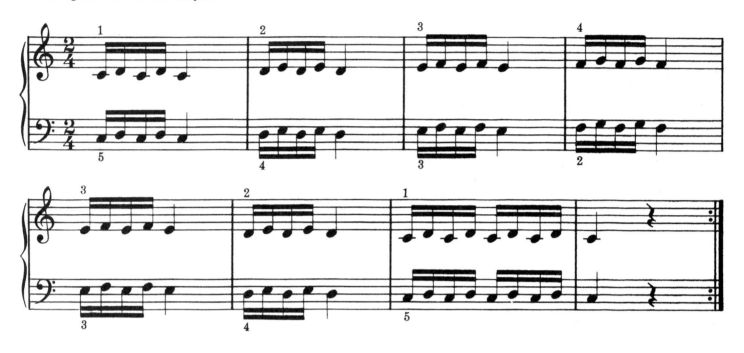

DOUBLE NOTE STUDIES

1.

Continue this pattern up the keyboard on the white keys.

2.

Continue this pattern up the keyboard on the white keys.

AUGMENTED TRIAD STUDIES

1.

2.

Transpose: A♭, E♭

3.

Transpose to other keys.

4.

DIMINISHED TRIAD STUDIES

DOTTED EIGHTH NOTE RHYTHM STUDIES

Transpose to other keys.

CLOUDY NIGHT

SYNCOPATED RHYTHM STUDIES

1.

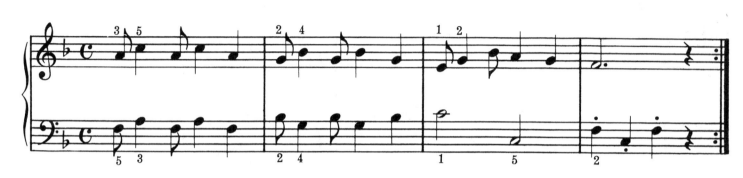

2.

IN OLD MEXICO

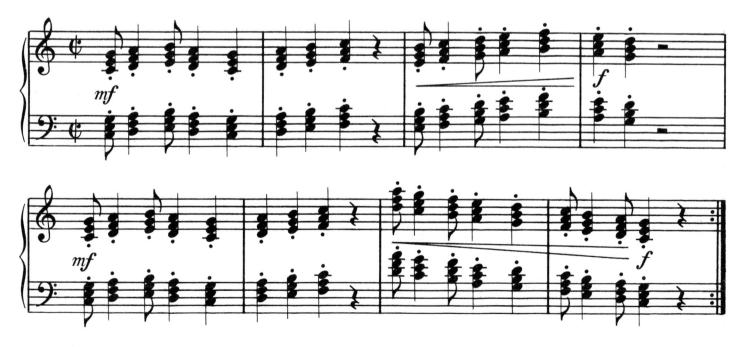

SLUR STUDY

CORNELIUS GURLITT

Grazioso

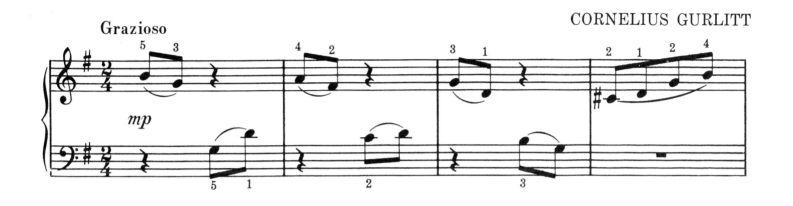

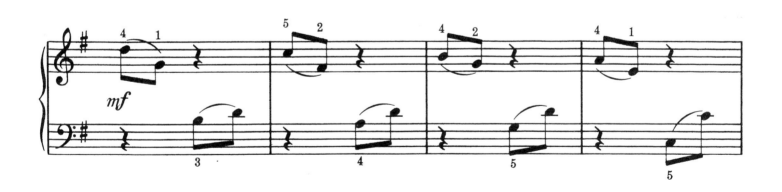

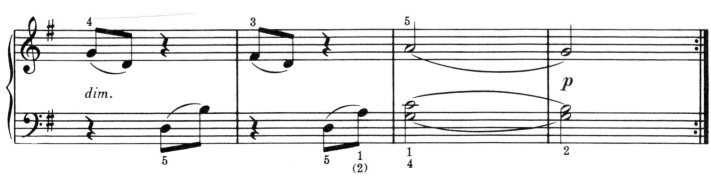

(2)

Gb MAJOR SCALE STUDIES

1.

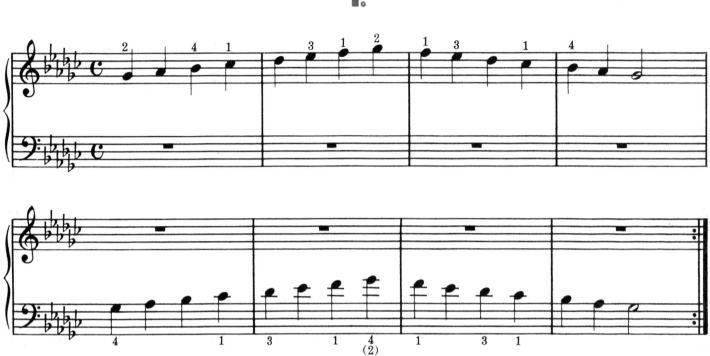

2.

3.

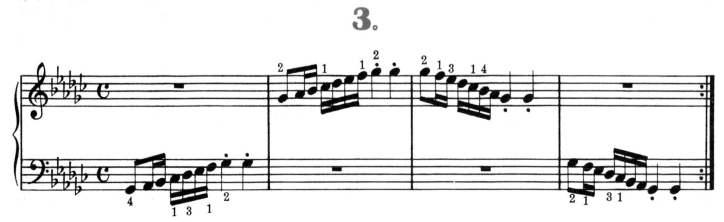

PRIMARY CHORDS IN G♭ MAJOR

WARM~UPS

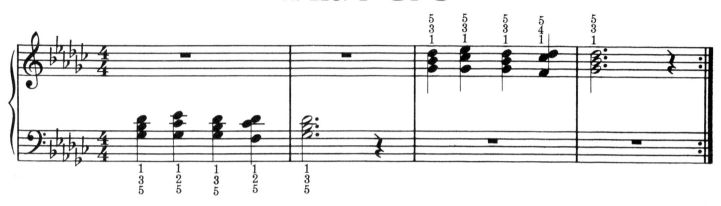

BLUE BIRD'S SONG

SWALLOWS IN FLIGHT

B♭ MAJOR SCALE STUDIES

1.

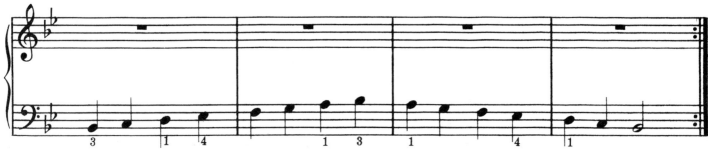

2.

3.

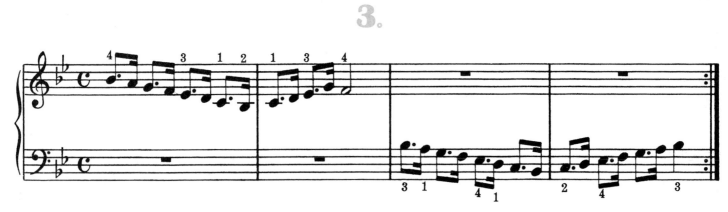

PRIMARY CHORDS IN B♭ MAJOR

WARM-UPS

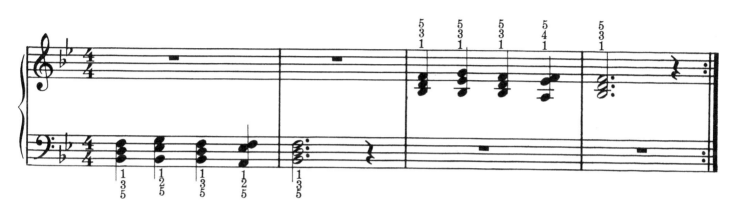

STEEPLECHASE

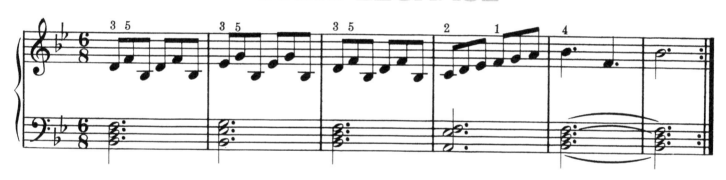

TWO O'CLOCK JUMP

B MAJOR SCALE STUDIES

1.

2.

PRIMARY CHORDS IN B MAJOR

WARM-UPS

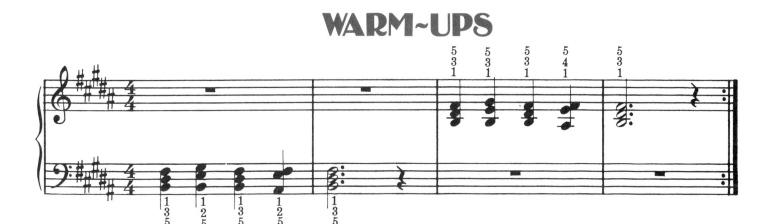

STRUMMING THE GUITAR

TICO TACO

CHROMATIC SCALE STUDY

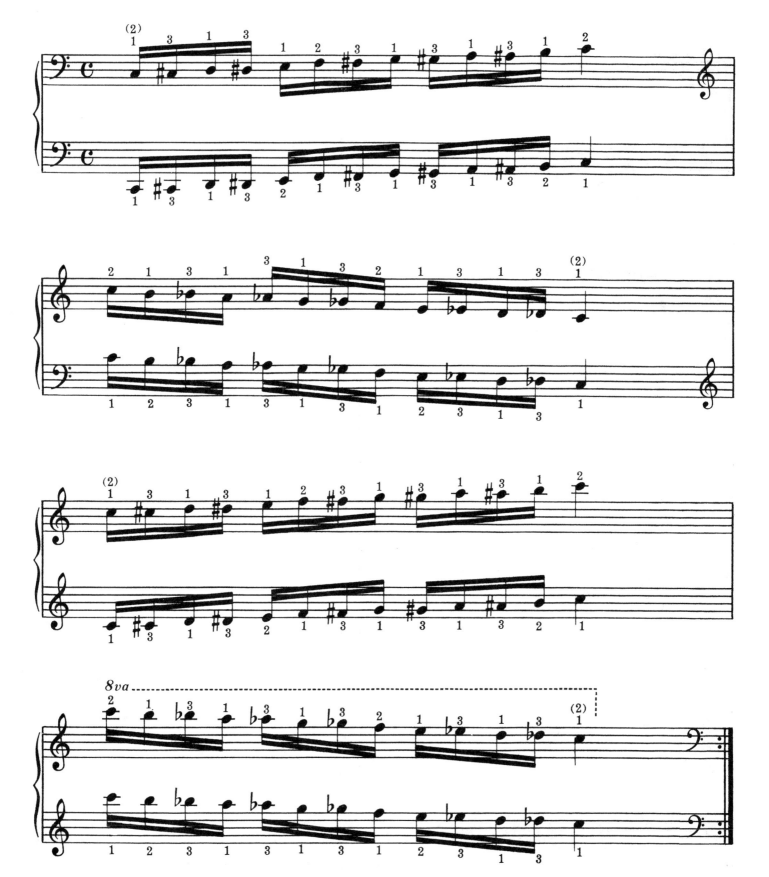

VELOCITY STUDIES

1.

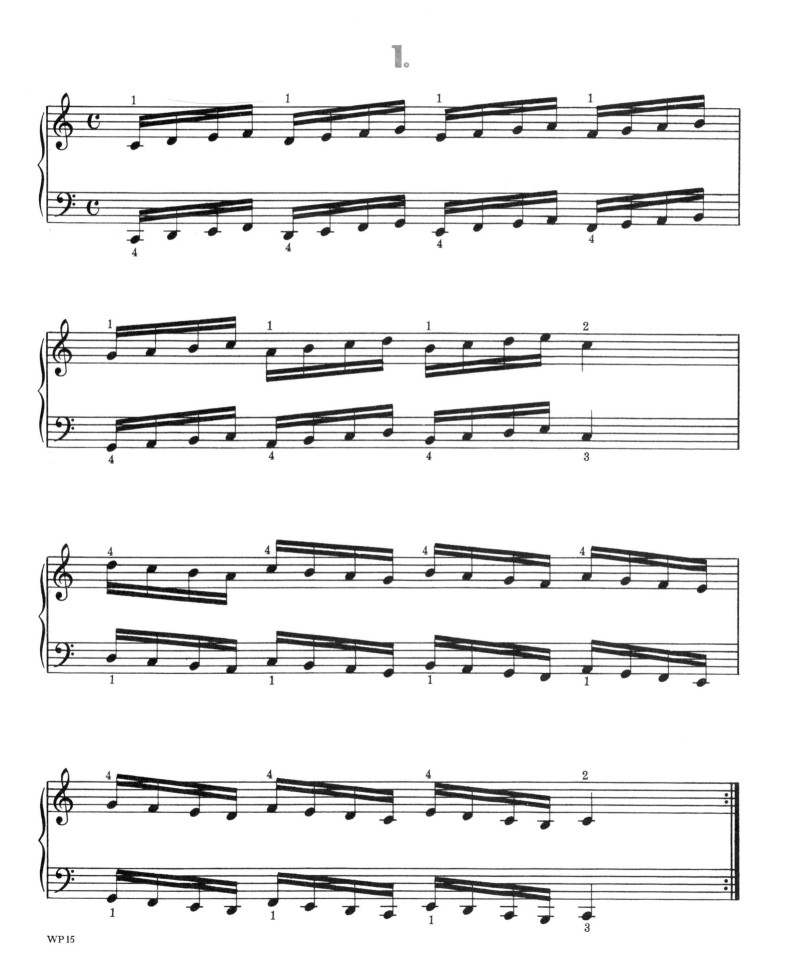

2.

Vivace

CARL CZERNY

ALBERTI BASS STUDY

WARM-UPS

Transpose to all other keys chromatically up the keyboard.

MR. ALBERTI'S SONG

VELOCITY STUDY

CARL CZERNY

HARMONIC MINOR SCALES
SHARP SCALES

HARMONIC MINOR SCALES
FLAT SCALES

TEACHER'S TECHNIC

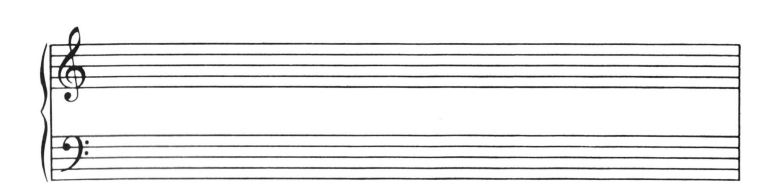

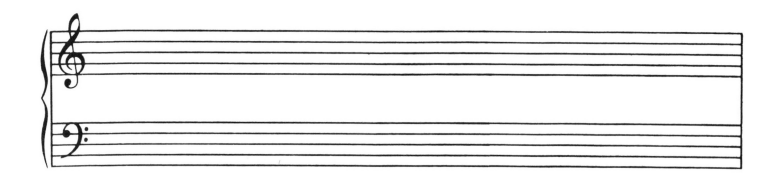